KIDS GET CODING

LEARN TO PROGRAM

Heather Lyons & Elizabeth Tweedale

WAYLAND

Contents

Getting started

Hi, I'm Data Duck! I'm here to help you learn all about computer programming.

A computer programmer is someone who writes programs that tell a computer what to do. It might be a game, or a shopping or searching program. This book is all about how to write computer programs.

DATA DUCK

Here are some key terms you will learn along the way. Try saying them out loud:

algorithm   objects   Java

program   syntax   co-ordinates

HTML   Python   Scratch

There are lots of activities in the book for you to try out. There are also some online activities for you to practise. For the online activities, go to **www.blueshiftcoding. com/kidsgetcoding** and look for the activity with the page number from the book.

What is a program?

A program is a list of instructions that tells a computer what to do. The list is known as an algorithm. It is written in a language that computers can understand called 'code'.

Human brains can connect meaning to instructions. For example, if someone in the playground said, "Go down the slide", we would understand that they mean for us to first walk up the steps, then sit and slide down.

However, a computer needs step-by-step instructions:

1. Walk to the steps.
2. Climb up the steps.
3. Sit at the top of the slide.
4. Slide down the slide.

Robot walk

Pretend a friend is a robot and write down a set of instructions that he has to follow to walk in a square.

Were your instructions clear enough? How could you have made them clearer?

DATA DUCK

Remember, the robot can only understand the exact instructions you give him: nothing more and nothing less.

Computer languages

Computers use different languages, just like humans all around the world do. Computers need the code for programs to be written in a language they can understand.

The language **HTML** is used to show web pages on the Internet. Computers use programs called Internet browsers (like Safari, Chrome or Internet Explorer) that understand HTML.

Scratch was written for kids to help them make their own computer programs. It uses blocks that we can snap together to build instruction lists.

Python is used to search for things on the Internet, and to organise all the information that a computer keeps in its memory.

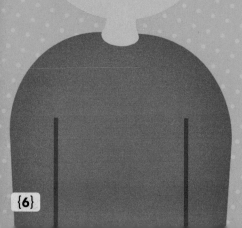

Java can be used to do some of the same things as Python. It can also be used for making computer games and apps.

DATA DUCK

A computer programmer needs to write the program in the best language for the job it needs to do. For example, Python is better at organising information and HTML is better at displaying it on a web page.

Mix and match

The way programmers use different computer languages is similar to the way people doing certain jobs need specific kinds of instructions. Can you match the instruction books below to the person who needs them?

Turn to page 23 to see the answers.

TASTY DISHES

MEDICAL DICTIONARY

FIXING CARS

HOW TO BUILD A HOUSE

Rules to follow

Computer languages use lots of symbols, letters and numbers. These fit together in a special way so that computers understand them.

A computer programmer needs to follow a set of rules known as the 'syntax' when writing a program. The syntax explains how the symbols, letters and numbers are put together. If anything is wrong in the code, the computer will get confused and will not know what to do.

```
print("Happy Birthday")
```

This Python code will write the words 'Happy Birthday' on the computer screen. For the text to appear on the screen, it must be in brackets and must have speech marks around it.

( )

brackets

" "

speech marks

DATA DUCK

When writing computer programs, it is very important for all the letters and symbols to be in the right place and that we don't leave anything out!

Hello, World!

The computer languages below will all show, "Hello, World!" on the screen. Which parts of the code are the same? Which symbols are used in the syntax of each language?

Turn to page 23 to see the answers.

HTML
```
<BODY>
<P>
"Hello, World!"
</P>
</BODY>
```

Python:
```
print("Hello, World!")
```

Java:
```
public class HelloWorld
 {
  public static void main(String[]args)
   {
    System.out.println("Hello, World!");
   }
 }
```

Scratch:
```
when clicked

say Hello, World! for 2 sec
```

Program bugs

Computer programs can sometimes go wrong. Problems with algorithms in a program are called 'bugs'. Finding and fixing the bugs is called 'debugging'.

The first step is to make sure everything in the code's syntax has been spelt correctly and that the right symbols have been used.

If we want to instruct a friend to 'Jump up and down' but the instruction says 'Lump op and don', our friend won't know what to do. The spelling mistakes are the bugs you need to fix.

Spot the difference!

Look at the two bits of Python code below. Can you spot the differences between them? Which one do you think is correct?

Turn to page 23 to see the answers.

DATA DUCK
Remember: there can be no characters missing, no extra characters and all the characters and lines of code need to be in the correct order!

```
import turtle
t = turtle.Pen()
t.forward(50)
t.left(90)
t.forward(50)
t.left(90)
t.forward(50)
t.left(90)
t.forward(50)
t.left(90)
```

```
import turtle
t = turtle.Pen()
t.forward(50)
t.left(90)
t.for(50)
t.left(90)
tforward(50)
t.left(90)
t.forward(50)
t.left90)
```

To tell the computer to draw things, Python uses the commands 'turtle' and 'Pen'. This helps it understand how to make shapes on screen.

IF, THEN and ELSE

Simple computer programs can also make complex decisions. A computer programmer will use 'IF statements' in the algorithm so that computers can make a decision.

We can use IF statements to decide what to wear in the morning:

IF it is rainy, THEN wear wellies.

We can use the same IF statement to tell the computer to choose between two options:

**IF it is rainy, THEN wear wellies,
ELSE wear sandals.**

Computer programmers use flow charts to plan decisions in programs. Here is one to help you decide what to wear today. This is based on the IF statement above.

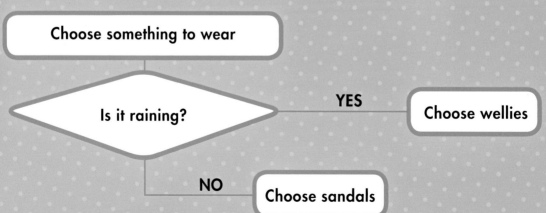

Choose something to wear

Is it raining?

YES → Choose wellies

NO → Choose sandals

School dinners

Look at the flow chart below. Can you decide which of the meal options below should be in the last two boxes?

Turn to page 23 to see the answers.

DATA DUCK
ELSE is the computer's word meaning 'otherwise'.

Choose your meal

Do I want a cold meal?

YES

Do I want a meat-free meal?

YES → Which meal fits here?

NO → Which meal fits here?

Cheese sandwich

Roast chicken

Macaroni and cheese

Ham and potato salad

Moving around

When computer programmers want to move characters or objects around a screen, they need to give location instructions as part of the algorithm.

The computer thinks of the screen like a map grid, so we need to tell the computer how the characters should move around the grid.

Let's use this treasure map to practise!

Treasure hunt

Data Duck has been blindfolded by pirates and needs your help to get to the treasure!

You can give him four instructions:
- Move left (by some spaces)
- Move right (by some spaces)
- Move up (by some spaces)
- Move down (by some spaces)

For example, to get to a duckling you would say:

Move right 5 squares
Move up 1 square

Turn to page 23 to see the answers.

Using the commands on page 14, see if you can complete these treasure challenges. Good luck, me hearties!

1. Get to the treasure (avoid the pirates and the snake).
2. Get to the treasure, collecting two ducklings along the way.
3. Get to the treasure, collecting two ducklings and going under the bridge.
4. Get to the treasure, collecting two ducklings and going across the bridge.

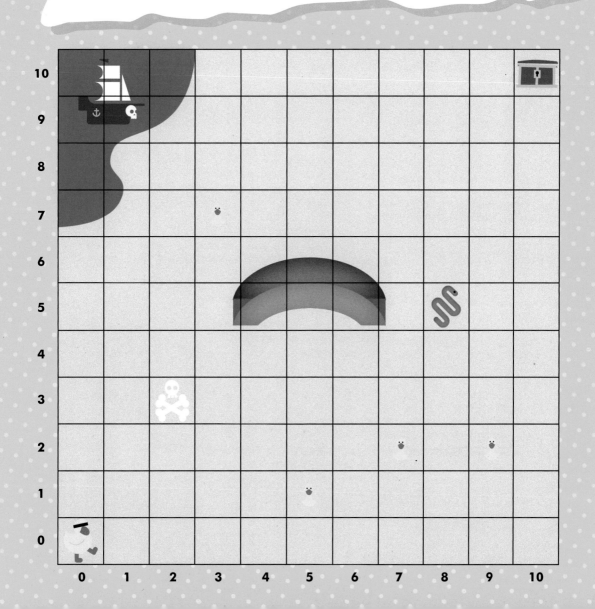

Giving instructions

When we write a program, we need to think carefully about what we need the program to do. The computer will need an instruction for every step that we can think of.

One of the instructions we need to give is where everything needs to go. Let's say we want to program a robot to feed our dog. We need to think through all the questions below so that we know all of the instructions to give the robot:

When does the dog eat?
How much does the dog eat?
What does the dog eat?
What does the dog eat out of?
Where does the dog eat?

When we have answered all the questions, we can start building an algorithm like the one below:

At 3pm, put one scoop of Bark-o's in plastic bowl on the kitchen floor.

If we leave anything out, the program will go wrong and the dog will be hungry!

BARK-O'S

Robots are computers, so they can't see and understand things the way we do. We need to tell the robot where to find everything. One of the ways we can tell the robot where to find things is with 'co-ordinates'.

Co-ordinates tell computers exactly where things are. Co-ordinates have two numbers: an 'x' number and a 'y' number. The 'x' numbers go across the map and the 'y' numbers go up and down the map. When giving locations, we always say the 'x' number first, then the 'y'.

Map the dog!

Here is a map of the dog, his bowl, his food and the robot.

The robot is at $x = -240, y = 0$

Where is the food?
Where is the bowl?
Where is the dog?

Turn to page 23 to see the answers.

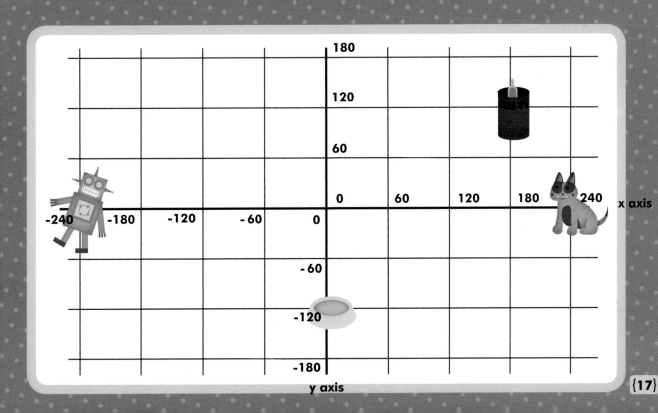

Writing a program

Now we know how to give a computer both detailed instructions and specific locations, we can write a program!

Apple picking

Data Duck has decided to go apple picking. Can you write down which of the steps on the right he needs to follow to pick three apples for his lunch?

Turn to page 23 to see the answers.

Go to x=120, y=-180

Go to x=-240, y=-60

Go to x=-180, y=120

Go to x=120, y=0

Pick up basket

Put apple in basket

Go to x=-120, y=60

Go to x=60, y=120

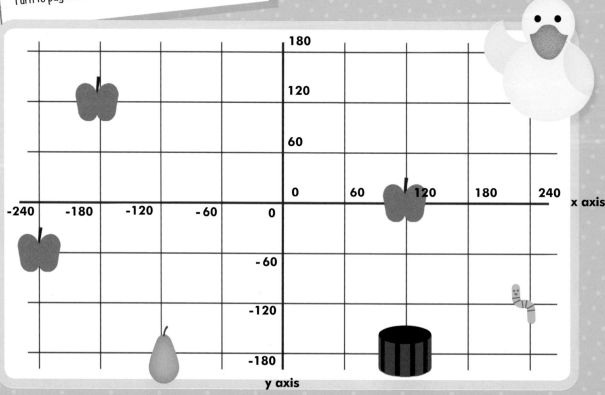

x axis

y axis

Go to **blueshiftcoding.com/kidsgetcoding** for more fun helping Data Duck go apple picking.

{18}

Sometimes, a computer needs to repeat a task over and over again. Instead of writing separate instructions for each task, a programmer can write algorithms in a 'loop'.

A loop tells the computer to repeat the activity inside it. The programmer can then tell the loop how many times to run. For example, we could tell a friend to skip. We could put those commands into a loop, so that our friend keeps skipping:

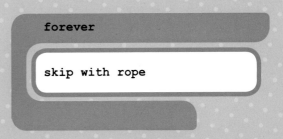

forever

skip with rope

With this loop, our friend will keep skipping forever. So, we also need to tell our friend to stop or change task. To do this, we need to add a 'condition'. This is an event which changes what happens.

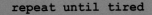

repeat until tired

skip with rope

DATA DUCK
We use conditions in everyday life, too. For example, we do all the sums in our maths homework, UNTIL there are no more sums to do.

Problem solving

When writing programs, a computer programmer needs to predict what the program is going to do, before the computer does it.

Look and find

Look at the following computer programs. What will the Python program draw? What will the boat do in the Scratch program?

Turn to page 23 to see the answers.

```
Go To (0,0)
Pen Down
Go To (2,-3)
Go To (-2,-3)
Go To (0,0)
Pen Up
```

Hint: try to work it out on graph paper.

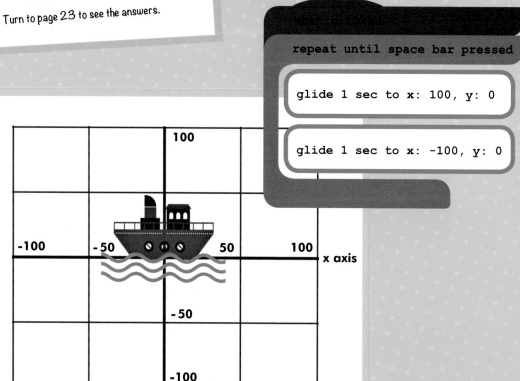

```
when clicked
repeat until space bar pressed
    glide 1 sec to x: 100, y: 0
    glide 1 sec to x: -100, y: 0
```

Bug hunter

It's also important for programmers to look at code and find bugs.

Look at the following computer programs. They are almost identical, but a few sneaky differences have appeared in the bottom program.

Can you spot these four bugs?

Turn to page 23 to see the answers.

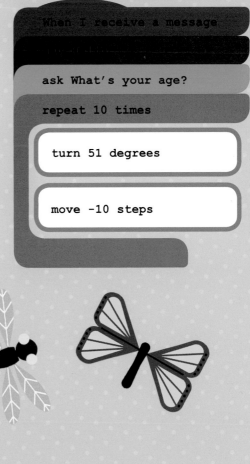

When I receive a message

ask What's your name?

forever

turn 15 degrees

move 10 steps

When I receive a message

ask What's your age?

repeat 10 times

turn 51 degrees

move -10 steps

Go to **blueshiftcoding.com/kidsgetcoding** for more debugging challenges.

Extension activities

Go to **blueshiftcoding.com/kidsgetcoding** for more fun activities and to practise:

- debugging
- writing programs
- predicting what programs will do
- co-ordinates

Words to remember

algorithm   a simple set of instructions that tells a computer what to do.

bug   a mistake in a computer programme.

code   the arrangement of instructions in a computer program.

condition   a factor that affects the instructions of a computer program.

co-ordinates   a system of finding a position. Co-ordinates are made up of two numbers or letters: one representing the horizontal position, the other the vertical position.

debugging   to find and remove bugs or errors in a computer programme.

loop   a series of steps with the final step connected to the first step, so the steps are repeated.

syntax   the structure of statements in a computer language.

variable   something that can be changed or adapted.

Activity answers

Page 7

Mechanic – Fixing Cars.
Cook – Tasty Dishes.
Builder – How to Build a House.
Doctor – Medical Dictionary.

Page 9

All the languages use the text Hello, World!
HTML uses brackets <> and forward slashes /.
Python uses brackets ().
Java uses a variety of brackets: [] {} ().
Scratch uses building blocks rather than symbols.

Page 11

The code on the left is correct. The righthand code is incorrect:

Line 6: uses 'for' instead of 'forward'
Line 8: there is no full stop before 'forward'.
Line 11: there is no open bracket before '90'.

Page 13

Cold meat-free meal: cheese sandwich.
Cold meal with meat: ham and potato salad.

Page 14

In the least number of moves:

Challenge 1: Move right 10 squares, move up 10 squares.

Challenge 2: Move up 2 squares, move right 7 squares, move right 2 squares, move right 1 square, move up 8 squares.

Challenge 3: Move right 9 squares, move up 2 squares, move left 2 squares, move left 2 squares, move up 8 squares, move right 5 squares.

Challenge 4: Move right 7 squares, move up 2 squares, move up 3 squares, move left 4 squares, move up 2 squares, move up 3 squares, move right 7 squares.

Page 17

The food is at x=180, y=120.
The bowl is at x=0, y=−120.
The dog is at x=240, y=0.

Page 18

You need the following steps:

Go to x=120, y=−180
Pick up basket
Go to x=120, y=0
Put apple in basket (this step will be needed three times)
Go to x=−240, y=−60
Go to x=−180, y=120

Page 20

The Python program will draw a triangle.
The boat in the Scratch program will glide back and forth across the screen.

Page 21

The third instruction asks 'What's your age?' not 'What's your name?'

The fourth instruction says 'repeat 10 times' not 'forever'.

The fifth instruction says 'turn 51 degrees' not 'turn 15 degrees'.

The sixth instruction says 'move −10 steps', not 'move 10 steps'.

Index

First published in Great Britain in 2016 by Wayland

Copyright © Wayland, 2016

All rights reserved.

Editor: Annabel Stones
Illustration: Alex Westgate
Freelance editor: Katie Woolley
Designer: Anthony Hannant (LittleRedAnt)

ISBN: 9780750297004
10 9 8 7 6 5 4 3 2 1

MIX
Paper from responsible sources
FSC
www.fsc.org
FSC® C104740

Wayland
An imprint of
Hachette Children's Group
Part of Hodder & Stoughton
Carmelite House
50 Victoria Embankment
London EC4Y 0DZ

An Hachette UK Company
www.hachette.co.uk
www.hachettechildrens.co.uk

Printed in China